RENO
GOLD

RENO ——— GOLD

The Unlimited Elite

PHILIP WALLICK

Published in 1989 by Osprey Publishing
Limited
59 Grosvenor Street, London W1X 9DA

© Phillip Wallick 1989

British Library Cataloguing in Publication
Data

Wallick, Phillip
   Reno gold: the unlimited elite
   1. Nevada. Reno. Air displays: Reno Air
   Races
   I. Title
   029.13'074'019355

ISBN 0-85045-923-0

Captions by Mike Jerram
Editor Dennis Baldry
Designed by David Tarbutt
Printed in Hong Kong

Front cover
#69 *Georgia Mae*, a P-51 Mustang,
flown by John Putman, was placed
fourth in the 1988 Gold Final

Back cover
Wiley Sanders' *Jeannie Too* was
flown by Ron Hevle in 1988

Title pages
Gold standard. Three of the most
highly modified P-51 Mustangs on
the current Unlimited air racing
scene pose in the shimmering heat
of the Reno ramp at the 1988
National Air Races. Left to right
Don Whittington's Griffon-engined
contra-rotating prop #8 *Precious
Metal*, John Dilley's North
American/Dilley 'Learstang' #19
Vendetta, and Scott Sherman's
#84 *Stiletto*, 1984 Gold
Champion

Right
*Here comes Fat Albert round turn
seven heading for eight and the
finishing straight*. . . Well, no, they
don't actually race Lockheed C-5A
Galaxies at Reno. This one was
part of the military participation at
the 1986 National Air Races.
Racing transports is not such a
bizarre idea. Former Unlimited racer
Clay Lacy and the late Herman
'Fish' Salmon once battled around
the pylons at Mojave in a DC-7
and Super Constellation

Appropriately decorated, *What Price Speed?* is a Bell P-63C Kingcobra raced at Reno 1979 by Mike Smith. As *Tipsy Miss* it had previously been owned by John Sandberg, and suffered a rash of problems with its specially modified Allison engine which ran on alcohol. The 'Cobra has since been restored to stock military configuration and is currently based at Duxford, England with warbird fanatic Stephen Grey's The Fighter Collection

Contents

Bearcat

Left
Here's a man just minutes away from becoming National Air Race Champion. Dallas-based Lyle Shelton, a former US Navy pilot and old campaigner at Reno, twice winner of the Unlimited Class Championship in 1973 and '75, saddles up for the start of the 1988 Gold Final

Main picture
Rare Bear heads for the start, trailed by John Maloney in the 1985 winner *Super Corsair*. Lyle Shelton bought the Bearcat as a derelict wreck for $2500 in the spring of 1968, restored it, installed a 3800 hp Wright R-3350 that 'spat out sand, leaves, trash, mice and bugs' the first time he ran it, and was placed fifth in the Championship Final in 1969. Shelton and the 'Cat have been regular competitors at Reno ever since

Above
Mustang crusher. Need we say more?

Ultimate Bear? Lockheed test pilot Darryl Greenamyer brought this F8F-2 Bearcat to the very first Reno Air Races in 1964 and led the Unlimited field throughout the final, but was disqualified for landing back at Reno Municipal Airport instead of at Sky Ranch, where the races were held. Note Senator Barry Goldwater's famous campaign emblem on the engine cowling. Greenamyer and the Bearcat returned to win Reno Gold for a record five successive times in 'The Reign of the Bear' between 1965–69, and again in 1971. Flying this aircraft, though in much modified form and renamed *Conquest 1*, Greenamyer averaged 483.041 mph in four runs over a three-kilometre course at Edwards AFB, California in August 1969 to break the world speed record for piston-engined aircraft set 30 years previously by Flugkapitan Fritz Wendel in a Messerschmitt Bf109R. *Conquest 1* now has a place of honour in the National Air and Space Museum, Washington, DC

This page and overleaf
A saddle on a motor
Burning dynamite for gas
With as little lifting surface
As will hike it off the grass

3000 leaping horses
With a feather for a girth
500 miles per hour
50 feet above the earth

The breed of man who rides her
Is an optimistic guy
With magic in his fingers
And a telescopic eye

Shelton's much modified Grumman
F8F-2 Bearcat #77 *Rare Bear*
wears this appropriate inscription
from an anonymous poet/air race
fan

Overleaf, left

Lyle Shelton leads his sizeable *Rare Bear* entourage in a rehearsal of the team's war cry: *Go Bear! Go Bear! Go Bear!* It did, and how . . .

Overleaf, right

Bear pit. #77's cockpit is workmanlike spartan. The purple control column is a legacy from *Rare Bear's* previous paint scheme. What's it like in there during a race? Shelton explains: 'When you get up above 440 mph it's a real hostile environment. It's hot—before we did a cooling job it used to get so hot that I could hardly keep my feet on the rudder pedals—and the noise and vibration and the clamour is just mind boggling. The stick forces are high, you need about all of your strength, two hands, to make turns, and you're just as busy as you can be and the adrenalin is high because you're just on the hairline edge of destruction of these engines. I used to be an amateur boxer, which is a pretty physical sport, but after a race I come back feeling like I've been in a five-round fight'

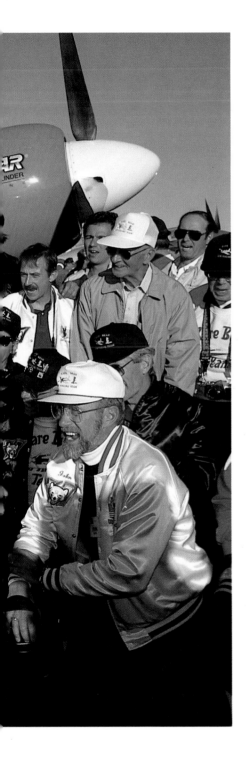

Main picture
After qualifying at a blistering new closed course record speed of 474.622 mph Shelton and *Rare Bear* quickly took the lead of the Gold Final pack, completing the eight lap course in 9:38.18 for a race average of 456.821 mph. 'I looked back at the Bearcat and he was about six feet behind me and then he just accelerated by me like a shot,' said second place man Rick Brickert, whose Super Sea Fury *Dreadnought* finished seven seconds behind Shelton. '*Rare Bear's* engine was as smooth a running engine as I've ever sat behind for a 3350,' said the victorious Shelton. 'That's not too smooth, but it was as smooth as any one of these round bangers has ever been. I had some more power left; we could have gone 475!'

Right
To the victor, the spoils. In this case a (very) large bonus cheque from new Unlimited race sponsors RJ Reynolds Tobacco Co. Shelton came away $40,437 richer after his win—no fortune when set against the immense cost of maintaining a competitive Unlimited air racer

Corsair

These pages
Ed Maloney's Chino-based Planes
of Fame Museum took a stock
F4U Corsair and grafted a 28
cylinder four-row Pratt & Whitney
R-4360 onto it, recreating the
shape and sound of the monster
F2G-1s in which Cook Cleland
and Ben McKillen dominated the
post-war Thompson Trophy races
at Cleveland before the fatal crash
in 1949 of Bill Odom's heavily
modified P-51C Mustang *Beguine*
put an end to Unlimited air racing
in the United States for 15 years

Overleaf
Numero Uno. A flatulent start for
Super Corsair during its debut at
the 1982 National Air Races, when
it was sponsored by Budweiser
beer and flown alternately by Steve
Hinton and the late Jim Maloney

Below
Cleaning up *Super Corsair's*
cockpit after an oil tank blow-up
during the victorious 1985
challenge

Right and overleaf, left
#1's 13 ft 6 in ex-Douglas

Skyraider prop disappears in a
shimmering arc as its crew chief
runs up the R-4360 prior to a heat
race at Reno 88. John Maloney
was in the hot seat. What was it
like the first time he flew the 3800
hp charger? 'I don't know. I was
too busy hanging on'

Above

John Maloney looks pensive as he waits to taxi out for the 1988 Gold Final. John qualified *Super Corsair* at 447.319 mph, but had finished only seven laps when Sunday's final ended. The name of brother Jim, who died in the crash of an antique Ryan trainer in which he was a passenger, is retained on #1 as a tribute

Right

When I grow up I want to be a race pilot like Daddy, but for now I'm content to be the tug driver. Young Steven Hinton, helped by mom Karen (née Maloney), puts in some pit work for uncle John at the 1988 races

Super Corsair team taking a bow in front of the grandstand after Steve Hinton's Gold victory in 1985. Hinton took the Championship at a record 438.186 mph after trailing Neil Anderson in the Sanders Super Sea Fury *Dreadnought* for the entire race. Anderson, distracted by a temperature gauge, cut the final pylon turn heading for the chequered flag and gave Hinton the sole Corsair victory in Reno's 25-year history. 'Winning in the Corsair was special because it's fun winning being the underdog . . . nobody expected us to do it and it was great, fantastic!' recalls Hinton

'It's a real sense of satisfaction and gratification when you work on these airplanes and compete, to get the maximum performance you can. . . There are moments of apprehension and wondering if you should be doing it, but when it's all over it's worth doing it. Winning is great'—Steve Hinton, 1978 and 1985 Champion

Mustang

'It compares to maybe a mission over Germany with a Hun on your tail and you're in big trouble. . . The speed is the fun thing. If you love speed, and I know I surely do, and it's racing, then that's what you're out there for, to enjoy all that speed and the competition, the show, and being centre stage. We're all nuts, you know. We've all got an ego problem, I guess, but that exhilaration! I think when you really get cranked up and going fast out there, competing with other people is about the most exhilaration I've ever had, unless it would be jumping out of an airplane with no parachute. You'd get real excited before you hit the ground'—Lefty Gardner, 1976 Champion

Many a Reno Gold contestant has had cause to be grateful to 'Bob' Hoover and his Mustang *Old Yeller*. Regarded by those who know as 'the pilot's pilot' Hoover attends every Reno air races to act as pace and safety pilot. On releasing the racers into the 'chute' for the start with his customary 'Gentlemen, you have a race,' Hoover pulls up to orbit high over the course like a guardian angel, ready to swoop alongside anyone calling a *Mayday*, sometimes handling as many as five emergencies at a time with calming, cooling words of often live-saving advice. 'I would like to think that I've made some small contribution to safety,' he says with typical modesty. 'I've talked pilots right down to the runway when they haven't been able to see for oil or smoke, and that's a nice feeling knowing that you've helped somebody save himself and his airplane.' When the former North American and Rockwell International test pilot isn't watching over his Unlimited charges, Hoover, now with Evergreen International, delights the Reno crowds with his aerobatic performances in a Shrike Commander and Sabreliner business jet

P-51 #5 had a long history of Reno racing, having previously been Chuck Hall's *Miss R J* and Gunther Balz's 1972 Gold winning *Roto-Finish Special*. Acquired by Ed Browning of Red Baron Flying Services in Idaho Falls in the early 1970s it underwent the most extensive Mustang transformation then undertaken. Browning, assisted by airframe gurus Bruce Boland and Pete Law and engine wizards Dave Zeuschel and Randy Scoville, replaced its Merlin engine with a Rolls-Royce Griffon 74 from a British Avro Shackleton maritime patrol aircraft, driving contra-rotating props, and made such fundamental changes to the airframe that the new designation RB-51 was considered appropriate. After making its Reno debut in 1975 it took two years to get *Red Baron* truly sorted, before Reno's 'winningest' pilot Darryl Greenamyer swept the field in 1977 to take his seventh Gold victory at a new race record speed of 430.70 mph. The following year a young man named Steve Hinton became the *Baron's* pilot and took the RB-51 to its second Reno victory, at the slower speed of 415.46 mph

Below
Red Baron in its original Merlin-engined form when flown by Mac McClain at Reno 74, just prior to its transformation into the RB-51

Below right
On 14 August 1979 Steve Hinton and the *Red Baron* broke Greenamyer's World Speed Record for piston-engined aircraft, streaking across a three-kilometre course at Tonopah, Nevada at 499.018 mph. Three weeks later Hinton, his Griffon engine sounding sick, trailed John Crocker's P-51 *Sumthin' Else* across the Gold Final finish line, pulled up and began a turn for an emergency landing on Stead Airport's Runway 26. He never made it. The *Baron's* engine seized, all six prop blades went to flat pitch, acting like an enormous airbrake, and the beautiful RB-51 slammed into the Lemon Valley and was totally demolished. Bob Hoover, circling above, believed that no one could have survived the wreck, but incredibly Steve was found alive, with multiple injuries, still strapped into his seat. 'I have a soft spot in my heart for the *Red Baron*,' says Hinton. 'I just really believed in the concept, that's all . . . if the *Red Baron* was still here today it would be the one to beat!'

Left
Gone, but not forgotten. Steve Hinton's brother John (right) and other members of the *Super Corsair* crew admire an immaculate scale model of *Red Baron*

Left
Bill 'Tiger' Destefani and Frank
Taylor built the beautiful #4 *Dago
Red* up in less than a year for the
1962 Reno Air Races, and were
well rewarded. Bakersfield
cropduster Ron Hevle qualified
Dago at 440.565 mph and took
Gold at 405.09 mph—the first time
that an all-new racer had ever
swept the board on its first time
out at Reno

This page
Dallas real estate developer Alan
Preston is the current owner of
Dago Red. Preston became the first
pilot to take part in all four Reno
classes—Unlimited, T-6,
International Formula Midget and
Biplane—in 1986, and took Gold
in IFM and Biplane in 1988. At
rest Dagos' cockpit looks cozy
enough, but going around the
course at 450 mph Preston says
'it's like being in a 450 mph
washing machine. It's noisy, it's
loud, it vibrates . . .' Preston is a
hard charger, but the Unlimited
Championship has so far eluded
him. 'Coming second is like kissing
your sister,' he says ruefully

These pages and overleaf, left
On 30 July 1983 Frank Taylor flew
Dago Red over a 15/25 kilometre
course at Mojave to set a piston-
engined World Speed Record at
517.06 mph

Above and overleaf
Rick Brickert had to call a *Mayday*
after *Dago Red's* Rolls-
Royce/Packard V-1650-9 threw a
conrod and caught fire during the
1984 Gold Final

Reflections in red. 'Tiger' Destefani returned to Reno 83 with yet another brand-new and radically modified Mustang, #7 *Strega*

Some broomstick! *Strega* is Italian
for 'witch', so #7 sports this
unusual line in pitot covers

Keeping the sponsor's name in the
public eye is all-important in the
megadollar world of Unlimited Air
Racing

After five years of disappointment the witch finally cast her spell for the *Strega* team in 1987 when Bill Destefani beat 1986 winner Rick Brickert in *Dreadnought* to set a new Gold race speed record of 452.559 mph. 'I knew at that time

we'd had a good run but I didn't think it'd be that fast,' recalls 'Tiger'. 'Had I known I could have whipped it up a bit more, but the next thing you know we jumped up with a record. My crew chief Bill Kerchenfaut radioed the time to me and I said, *Aw bullshit!* I knew he was lyin' and tryin' to pull my leg . . .'

Engine preparation is all important. In military use a Mustang's Merlin would be operated at 3000 rpm and 61 inches of boost. At Reno seeing 120 inches on the boost

gauge is not unusual. Sadly *Strega* didn't manage the right brew of tongue of bat and eye of newt in 1988. Oil starvation resulted in a blown Merlin during a qualifying round

Preceding page and this page
Since his first rookie race in 1973
World Airlines captain John
Crocker has been a popular and
competitive racer at Reno. On his
first appearance with #6 *Sumthin'*
Else in 1976 he was one of three
pilots to break the qualifying speed
record on three successive days
and became National Air Race
Champion in the eventful Gold
Final of 1979, which he won at
422.30 mph. At Reno 88 *Sumthin'*
Else appeared in this attractive
colour scheme, but was relegated
to second place in the so-called
'Super Stocks' Silver Final after
Crocker incurred a 16-second
penalty for cutting pylon 1 on
lap 4

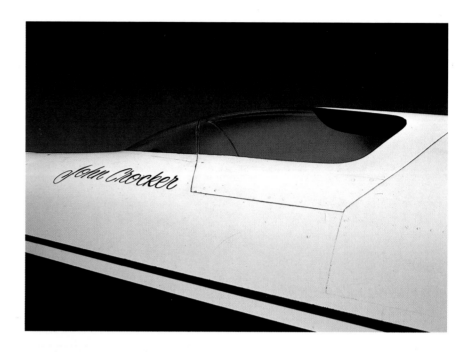

Ken Burnstine brought *Foxy Lady* to Reno in 1974, fresh from a rebuild from stock P-51D configuration by Leroy Penhall's Fighter Imports at Chino, California. The sleek Mustang arrived in sinister all-black colour scheme and had all of its attractive decoration added by hand in the pit area. To no avail, sadly. Engine problems prevented *Foxy Lady* from qualifying, but for consolation Burnstine took his stock P-51 *Miss Suzi Q* to victory in the Gold. After Burnstine's death at Mojave in 1975 John Crocker bought *Foxy Lady* and she became the 1979 Gold Champion *Sumthin' Else*

Preceding pages, opposite and below
The Whittington brothers from Fort Lauderdale, Florida spent five years putting together #09 *Precious Metal*, which despite the name shares only the tail cone of their previous Mustang, most of this aircraft being brand new. Like *Red Baron*, *Precious Metal* is powered by a Rolls-Royce Griffon engine driving contra-rotating propellers and is arguably the most spectacular looking Mustang yet

Left
Don Whittington latches *Precious Metal's* canopy in preparation for the Gold Final, but . . .

Preceding page and above
Déjà vu. Like the *Red Baron* nine years previously the Griffon-engined Mustang ended up in the dirt of Reno's Lemon Valley, but fortunately Whittington walked away. 'Just as Hoover called "Gentlemen, you have a race," I pushed it up a little more. I was adding power, and just at that point Hoover had already pulled up and we were coming up on the Interstate, that's when it happened.

The propeller governor failed and the blades went the other direction The rpms went to 5500 or 6000 blew the spinner apart. My first thought was that I was going to have to get out because it was shaking rather badly. I started to do that, but that wouldn't work because I realised that I was going too slow. I had already slowed down to roughly 130 indicated. I looked down and could see I was over a populated area, so I pushed

everything back up, and it didn't shake any worse. I went ahead and turned the mag switch back on and it fired. I gave it a little throttle to get a little airspeed going forward, because it was coming down, and I mean it was coming *straight down!*' Whittington successfully bellied *Precious Metal* onto the dry lake bed, and vowed to have it flying again before year's end

Spectre and #44 *Leeward Air Ranch Special*, seen here in 1983 and 1984 are one and the same aircraft. It has the longest pedigree in Unlimited racing . . .

. . . catalogued on the engraved
landing gear leg cover of the
repainted #9. As #77 *Galloping
Ghost* the then stock Mustang took
part in the post-war Thompson,
Sohio and Tinnerman Trophy races
at Cleveland, before emerging at
the revived Reno National Air
Races as Cliff Cummins' radically
modified #69 *Miss Candace*, and
later Wiley Sanders' *Jeannie*

At Reno 88 Jimmy Leeward, a property developer from Ocala, Florida, qualified the *Leeward Air Ranch Special* fourth fastest at 457.078 mph, but during Gold group Heat 3A on Saturday he called a *Mayday*. Finding an unauthorised fuel truck blocking the emergency runway, Leeward set his Mustang down on a dirt road, bounced into the sagebrush and damaged his propeller

69

These pages and overleaf, left
In 1988 the patriotic red, white and blue #11 *Miss America* was the mount of veteran Reno racer Chuck 'Always Second' Hall, whose duels in his P-51 #5 *Miss R J* with Darryl Greenamyer's Bearcat were a feature of the early Reno races in the 1960s

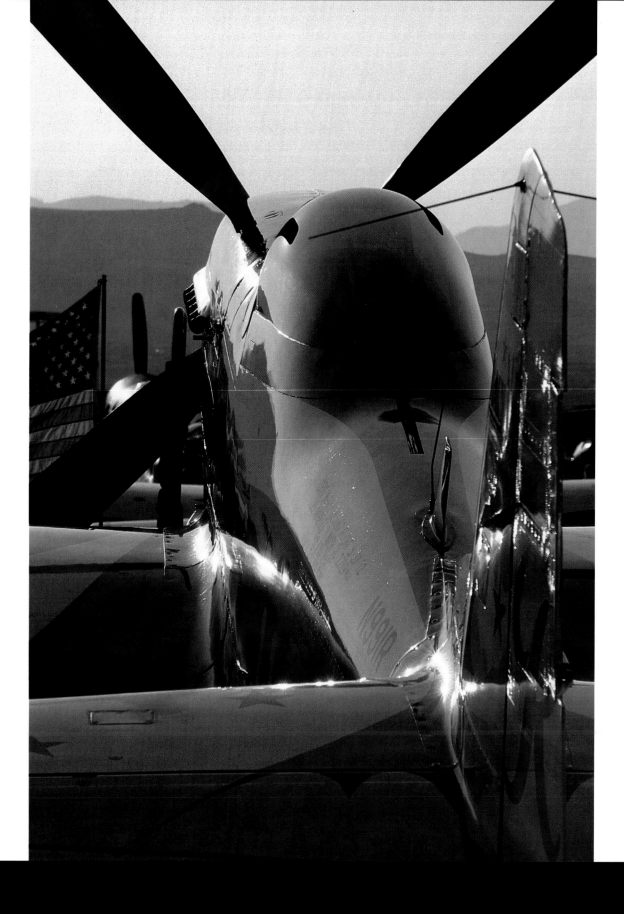

Above
Canadian pilot Bud Granley flew
the former Howie Keefe Mustang
Miss America at Reno in 1985

Is it a Learjet? Is it a Mustang?
Actually, it is a bit of both. John
Dilley's North American/Dilley
#19 *Vendetta* was among the
most eagerly anticipated
contestants at Reno in 1988.
Dilley, a fixed-base operator from
Fort Wayne, Indiana, mated the
wing (*sans* tiptanks) and horizontal
stabiliser of a Learjet 23 bizjet to a
Mustang fuselage and fin

Vendetta, dubbed Learstang by race aficionados, is powered by a Jack Hovey-prepared Rolls-Royce Merlin 622. During tests prior to arrival at Reno Dilley reported a true airspeed of 475 mph at 80 inches of boost. 'It runs excellently, you can turn it on a dime. I did some "combat" with other Mustangs and I could turn right inside them every time. . . It rolls just like a Pitts Special. You just touch the stick and it starts rolling. Climbing out of Reno here at 5000 feet altitude I get a 4600 feet per minute rate of climb'

These pages and overleaf
A backfire prior to qualifications runs kept *Vendetta* out of the running in 1988, but John Dilley is optimistic about its future. 'I feel the aircraft has definite potential. It is just at its starting point and it's fast already. I feel it will easily go around the pylons at 470.'

Right
Aaaaargh! Frustration shows on John Dilley's face at another malfunction. 'We work on it a week for every hour we fly. Since it takes seven hours to get to Reno, it'll be seven weeks before we're ready to race,' he had said only half jokingly before coming to Reno

Texas cropduster and Confederate Air Force founder member Lefty Gardner puts his working skills to good effect rounding the Reno pylons in his P-38 *White Lit'nin* and P-51D *Thunderbird* lower than the competition. 'I'm real comfortable flying low to the ground . . . when you get cranked up and going fast, you get on your toes and really become alert, all your faculties are there, you're not thinking about some other type of thing, like girls. . .' Is it true that Lefty once taxied back to the pits with sagebrush on his wingtip? 'It's true. I did hit a sagebrush in 1980, but it wasn't *that* short. The bush was at least 10 or 12 feet tall!' Lefty and *Thunderbird* were National Champions in 1976 at 379.61 mph

These pages and overleaf
Gary Levitz flew his stock P-51D
Mustang #38 *Miss Ashley* to first
place in the Gold Final at Reno 88,
clocking 381.347 mph. Levitz,
President of a retail furniture
company, has been a regular Gold
contender at Reno in a P-38
Lightning and Mustangs. He finds
pylon racing relaxing. 'I'd rather fly
all day around the pylons than I
would fly through the Phoenix
Terminal Control Area once. I get
more stressed out just going to
work in the week than I do racing'

Bill Rheinschild's eye-hurting polished metal P-51D #45 *Risky Business* was the 1988 Silver winner at 414.495 mph—faster than the back markers in the Gold final

Seen from the cockpit of Dennis Sanders' Sea Fury #924, here's how it looks as they're running into the chute . . .

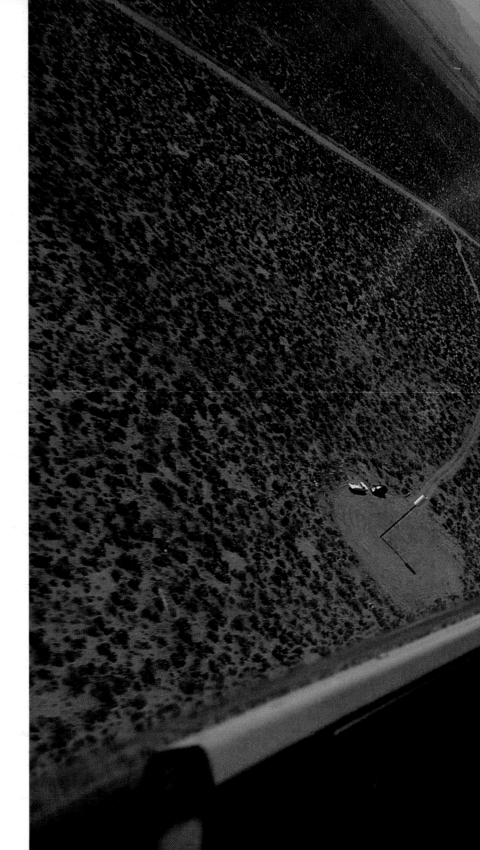

. . . and on the course: hot, noisy, bumpy, G-loaded, with fuel, oil and adrenalin pumping about equal as you rack it around the pylon, already looking ahead for the next turn

92

These pages and overleaf, left
Reno veterans. The late E D
Weiner's chequerboard #49 placed
second in the 1967 Gold Final
ahead of Clay Lacy's #64,
popularly known as the 'Purple
People Eater'. Lacy and the
lavender-hued Mustang won the
Gold event at Reno 1970 at
387.342 mph

Right and overleaf, left Wiley Sanders' #69 *Jeannie*, formerly *Galloping Ghost* and *Miss Candace* took Gold in successive years— 1980 in the hands of Mac McClain at 433.01 mph, and in 1981 with Skip Holm at 431.29 mph after qualifying at a record 450.09 mph. Looking for a hat trick in 1982, *Jeannie* suffered two blown engines, the second when the prop governor failed during a qualification run. In the ensuing runaway the rpms were thought to have gone over 7000. With *Jeannie* shrieking like a banshee, Holm pulled up vertically to trade some speed for altitude, lost 300 knots in an instant without gaining much height and made an immaculate deadstick landing in near blind conditions because of oil covering the windshield. *Jeannie* now races as the *Leeward Air Ranch Special*

Same colour scheme, same race
number, different airplane.
Jeannie's replacement in the Wiley
Sanders Racing Team stable was
Georgia Mae, seen here being
buffed up for the 1988 Gold Final
as owner Sanders (right) looks on.
Pilot John Putman placed fourth at
408.287

These pages and page 103 bottom

Stiletto was developed by Alan Preston, now owner of *Dago Red*, and is quite different in concept from other 'Super Mustangs'. The P-51's characteristic belly cooling scoop has been eliminated and replaced by flush inlets in the wing leading edges and computer-controlled spraybars. Note dramatically cropped wings. Skip Holm flew *Stiletto* to victory in the 1984 Gold event at 437.62 mph. 'I like flying Mustangs, and my favourite would have to be *Stiletto*. *Stiletto* was honed to be the closest to what you would want in a racing Mustang,' says Holm. '*Jeannie* is a great airplane . . . but *Stiletto* took the refinement a step further and took care of some of the problems with *Jeannie*, but we also probably made the airplane more difficult to maintain and fly.' New owner/pilot Scott Sherman, who runs an aircraft sales company in North Palm Beach, Florida reports: 'It's a bit like flying a jet. It's a real nice flying machine, but when you're running at high power you know that you're sitting behind that hand grenade. You're just playing the odds.' The odds were against him in 1988. Sherman *Maydayed* out of the Gold Final

'It's not my money, it will never be my money. That's the other secret—never own your own airplane, never be responsible for a piece of metal out there, never take it seriously. The minute you do you're in big trouble. . . Test flying these racers is always a judgement call by your peers. The guys who like you say you have big balls. The guys that don't particularly like you say you are an idiot. And they're both right. . .'—Skip Holm, 1981 and 1984 Champion

Left
Rattlesnake's eye view of race preparations for Scott Sherman's Mustang #84 *Stiletto*

Below
Stiletto gets a wax job prior to the 1988 final

Above
Something borrowed . . . *Stiletto* briefly wore *Dago Red's* rudder at the 1986 races, but failed to finish in the Gold event, while the donor placed fourth

103

Sea Fury

Frank Sanders, long-time exponent of British Hawker Sea Fury, hit upon the idea of re-engining the 2480 hp Bristol Centaurus-powered fighter with a 3800 hp Pratt & Whitney R-4360-63A 'corncob' and first brought the meticulously prepared *Dreadnought* to Reno in 1983. Flown by General Dynamics famed F-16 test pilot Neil Anderson in his rookie racing year, #8 *Dreadnought* almost loafed through qualification at 446.39 mph and took Gold at 425.24 mph after a ding-dong battle with Rick Bricket in P-51 *Dago Red*, who had to call a *Mayday* on Lap 6

Dreadnought, formerly a two-seat fighter/trainer with the Burmese Air Force, is towed out to the run-up area at Reno 88, past the Sanders Racing Team's stock Sea Fury #924, flown by Frank's son Dennis. Experienced though he was in flying powerful warbirds, Frank admits that the boost in performance going from racing a stock Sea Fury to *Dreadnought* surprised him. 'There's the amount of physical effort it takes at higher speeds, and how much less time there is even to look at the instruments—you're only straight and level for ten seconds or so, and you can only sneak a look at your instruments to check your airspeed and temps and fuel flows'

Airline pilot Rick Brickert took over from Neil Anderson as *Dreadnought's* pilot in 1986 and took Gold that year at 434.488 mph. In 1988 he qualified third fastest at 458.920 mph and chased Gold winner Lyle Shelton all the way to the line, with a race speed of 451.202 mph. Brickert, who dreamed of flying at Reno ever since his sister brought him to the races at the age of 13, is impressed by the reliability of the 'corncob' Sea Fury and its lack of 'cockpit complexity'. 'Coming down the chute I close the doors up, at 40 inches of boost I turn on the ADI, turn on the cylinder head spray system and go all the way up. After that it's just a question of monitoring it while I concentrate on racing'

'The one thing I take seriously is that you can get seriously killed'—Rick Brickert, 1986 Champion

Opposite and above
Lloyd Hamilton's 'corncob' Sea Fury #15 *Furias* has undergone continual refinement since its Reno debut as *Head Gorilla* in 1983 but has so far been denied Gold

Left
Furias qualified at 424.081 mph in 1988 and placed fifth in the Gold Final after overtaking John Maloney in *Super Corsair*

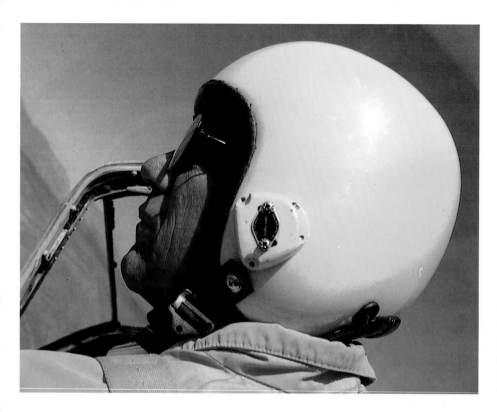

Lloyd Hamilton rounding a pylon on the Reno course. Turbulence is an ever present problem in pylon racing. 'I took a bump the other day. I have no idea what the G loading was, and I keep myself strapped in good, but my helmet hit the canopy so hard that I thought I'd busted it. Honest to God, when I looked up I didn't believe it was still there,' says Hamilton of an incident during the 1988 races. Like most Gold racers Hamilton is happiest in the close company of his peers, and enjoys the great camaraderie of Unlimited racing, but 'There's no such thing as camaraderie once the pace plane pulls up. If you are not aggressive, you're not out there to win'

This page and below left
Lloyd Hamilton also owns the stock Sea Fury #16 *Baby Gorilla*, a past Gold participant raced in 1988 by Santa Rosa, California corporate pilot C J Stephens. *Baby Gorilla* wears authentic Royal Australian Navy colours, but its fuselage roundel was modified for 1988 by the addition of race sponsors Camel Cigarettes' logo. Stephens placed third in the Bronze event at 386.869 mph

Electrical contractor and long-time T-6 racer Jim Mott brought his new Sea Fury #42 *Super Chief* to Reno 88, fresh from rebuild by Aero Traders at Chino, but did not qualify. *Super Chief* is powered by a Bristol Centaurus 173 engine from a Royal Air Force Blackburn Beverley transport, driving a cut-down, four-blade propeller from a Bristol Britannia airliner

High steppin'. Putting a shine on Canadian Jerry Jane's mirror-bright Sea Fury #20 *Cottonmouth* keeps his crew on their toes . . . literally. Beneath that standard Sea Fury cowling lies a Wright R-3350-26 driving a four-blade Hamilton Standard propeller from an F4U-4 Corsair. In pilot John Muszala's hands *Cottonmouth* placed second in the Bronze event at Reno 88, clocking 374.980 mph

Tsunami

Left and overleaf
Minneapolis industrialist John Sandberg's *Tsunami*, seen here in 1986, is the only wholly original design Unlimited racer to have appeared at Reno in its 25-year history. Sandberg, who has been involved with the preparation of racers for a quarter of a century, set out to build the world's fastest piston-engined airplane. He enlisted the help of designer Bruce Boland, a Lockheed aerodynamicist whose influence can be seen in many Unlimited racers, along with Pete Law, Ray Poe and Tom Emery. Work began in 1979 and *Tsunami* (Japanese for tidal wave) first flew in 1986 and made its Reno debut that year in the hands of Steve Hinton, who qualified at 435 mph but was forced to pull out of the Gold Final after his engine blew

Below
Wide-eyed with wonder—*Tsunami* fabrication man Don Pennington Designer Boland's brief was to create the smallest possible airframe to fit behind the engine, which is built up from a Rolls-Royce/Packard V-1650-7 crankcase and two-stage blower with heavy duty crankshaft and cylinder head and bank assemblies from the Merlin 624 and 724 series used on post-war transport aircraft. Maximum racing output is around 3600 hp at 105 inches of boost. Boland certainly succeeded in his task. *Tsunami* has a frontal area 77 per cent of that of a stock P-51, and at 146 square its wing area is only 60 per cent of the Mustang's

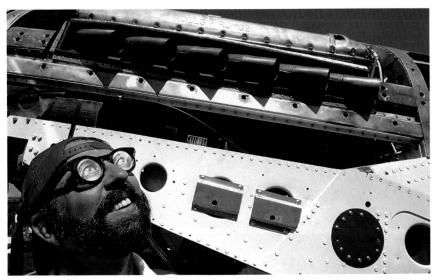

Tsunami came to Reno 88 much modified from previous years. The JRS team rebuilt the airframe, replacing the entire back end with a magnesium structure, resulting in a weight reduction of some 700 pounds. New water and oil cooling systems, new inlet scoop and outlet door, more downthrust for the engine, increased fin and rudder area, new ten foot diameter propeller, trimmable stabiliser and revised aileron controls were just some of the modifications which went into the airplane to make it fly and race better. Pilot Hinton expressed himself well pleased with #18's handling. He qualified second fastest in the Unlimited field at 470.899 mph, pipped *Dreadnought* to the line in Saturday's Heat 3A, but suffered a coolant valve failure in the Gold Final and was forced to throttle back, placing third at a race speed of 429.947 mph. An attempt on the world piston engined speed record is in prospect for 1989

Left
'There I was, 470 on the clock and
. . .' Steve Hinton uses some body
language to explain to
Dreadnought pilot Rick Brickert
how *Tsunami* beat him and set a
new course record of 462.218 mph
in the Gold Heat 3A on Saturday,
Reno 88

Yak-11